ADMINISTRATIVE AND TAX LAW IN USE

Master 300+ Administrative And Tax Law Terms And Phrases Explained With Examples In 10 Minutes A Day.

JOHNNY CHUONG

Copyright © 2018

All rights reserved.

ISBN: 9781729107072

TEXT COPYRIGHT © JOHNNY CHUONG

All rights reserved. No part of this guide may be reproduced in any form without permission in writing from the publisher, except for brief quotations used for publishable articles or reviews.

Legal Disclaimer

The information contained in this book and its contents is not designed to replace any form of medical or professional advice; and is not meant to replace the need for independent medical, financial, legal, or other professional advice or services that may be required. The content and information in this book have been provided for educational and entertainment purposes only.

The content and information contained in this book have been compiled from sources deemed reliable, and they are accurate to the best of the Author's knowledge, information, and belief. However, the Author cannot guarantee its accuracy and validity and therefore cannot be held liable for any errors and/or omissions. Further, changes are periodically made to this book as needed. Where appropriate and/or necessary, you must consult a professional (including but not limited to your doctor, attorney, financial advisor, or other such professional) before using any of the suggested remedies, techniques, and/or information in this book.

Upon using this book's contents and information, you agree to hold harmless the Author from any damages, costs, and expenses, including any legal fees potentially resulting from the application of any of the information in this book. This disclaimer applies to any loss, damages, or injury caused by the use and application of this book's contents, whether directly or indirectly, whether for breach of contract, tort, negligence, personal injury, criminal intent, or under any other circumstance.

You agree to accept all risks of using the information presented in this book.

You agree that by continuing to read this book, where appropriate and/or necessary, you shall consult a professional (including but not limited to your doctor, attorney, financial advisor, or other such professional) before using any of the suggested remedies, techniques, or information in this book.

INTRODUCTION

Thank you and congratulate you for downloading the book *"Administrative and Tax Law in Use: Master 300+ Administrative and Tax Law Terms and Phrases Explained with Examples in 10 Minutes a Day."*

With a clear, concise, and engaging writing style, Johnny Chuong will provides you over 300 administrative and tax law terms and phrases that help you expand your legal words list with a practical understanding of administrative and tax law topics such as *constitution, human rights, complaint, denunciation, administrative procedure, personal income tax, tax-exempt incomes* **and much much more**. If you'd like to increase your wide range of legal vocabulary as well as enhance your knowledge of *administrative and tax law*, then this book may be the most important book that you will ever read.

As the author of the book, Johnny Chuong promises this book will be an invaluable source of legal reference for professionals, international lawyers, law students, business professionals and anyone else who want to improve their use of legal terminology, succinct clarification of legal terms and have a better understanding of administrative and tax law. This book provides you with a comprehensive and highly practical approach in legal contexts, the world of administrative and tax law related to *constitution, human rights, complaint, denunciation, administrative procedure, personal income tax, tax-exempt incomes, etc*. All legal terms and phrases are well written and explained clearly in plain English.

Take action today and start mastering 300+ essential administrative and tax law terms and phrases explained with examples tomorrow!

Thank you again for purchasing this book, and I hope you enjoy it.

ADMINISTRATIVE LAW

Sovereign [Adjective]: to be independent and not under the authority of any other country.

China is an independent and sovereign country.

All acts against the independence, sovereignty, unity of the Fatherland shall be severely punished.

The people's armed forces shall protect the independence, sovereignty, unity and territorial integrity of the Fatherland.

Legislative [Adjective]: relating to or having the power to make or pass laws.

Executive [Noun]: relating to or having the power to put laws into effect.

Judicial [Noun]: relating to the judgments made in a court of law or the administration of justice.

The exercise of the judicial powers, executive and legislative.

Democracy [Noun]: a state governed by the majority of its members.

Direct democracy.

Exercise democracy and promote social consensus.

Human rights [Noun]: rights that are believed to belong justifiably to each individual.

The State shall recognize, respect, protect and guarantee human rights and citizens' rights.

National security [Noun]: a country's ability to protect itself from the threat of attack or violence.

Human rights and citizens' rights may not be limited unless solely in case of national defense, national security.

A citizen has the obligation to participate in the safeguarding of national security and social order and safety.

Inviolability [Noun]: the state of being inviolable;

Everyone has the right to inviolability of body or private life.

Freedom of belief and religion.

People have the right to be respected and protected the freedom of belief and religion.

Gender equality [Noun]: human rights that are treated equally between men and women.

Female and male citizens have equal rights in all fields.

Gender discrimination is prohibited.

A complaint [Noun]: a written or spoken statement that a situation is unsatisfactory or unacceptable.

Everyone has the right to lodge complaints about illegal acts of agencies, organizations or individuals.

Competent agencies shall receive and resolve complaints and denunciations.

Denunciation [Noun]: the act of accusing someone in public that he/she has done something wrong or illegal.

The right to complaint or denunciation.

The settlement of complaints and denunciations.

Social security [Noun]: monetary assistance to people with an inadequate or no income (retired persons, the disabled, the poor, etc.)

Citizens have the right to social security.

The State shall create equal opportunities for citizens to develop the social security system.

Administrative procedures [Noun]: a set of rules that govern the procedures for managing an organization.

The Law on Administrative Procedures.

Settling complaints and denunciations in administrative procedures.

Provision of documents and evidences in administrative procedures.

Equality in rights and obligations in administrative procedures.

Administrative procedure-conducting persons.

Administrative procedure-conducting persons include:

a/ Examiners, chief procurators, and procurators.

b/ Chief justices, people's assessors, judges, verifiers, and clerks of courts;

Administrative procedure-conducting agencies.

Administrative procedure-conducting agencies include courts and procuracies.

Powers and responsibilities of procedure-conducting agencies.

Administrative procedure participants.

Administrative procedure participants include:

   a)   Involved parties, representatives of involved parties;

   b)   Defense counsels of the lawful rights and interests of involved parties;

   c)   Witnesses, expert witnesses;

   d)   Interpreters.

Administrative procedure participants may use spoken and written languages of their nations.

Instituting a lawsuit: to sue, bring suit, bring to litigation.

Order and procedures for instituting lawsuits.

Administrative [Adjective]: relating to administration.

Administrative case [Noun]: a case between a person on the one side and state authority from the other.

The settlement of administrative cases involving foreign elements.

Examination and handling of legal documents and acts related to administrative cases.

Participation of people's assessors in the trial of administrative cases.

Diplomatic [Adjective]: involving relations between the governments of different countries.

Consular [Adjective]: relating to a consul or a consulate.

Privilege [Noun]: a special right, or advantage granted to a particular person or group of people.

International organizations eligible for diplomatic or consular privileges.

Administrative decision [Noun]: a document issued by a state administrative agency on a specific matter in administrative management activities.

The administrative decision over which a lawsuit is instituted.

The plaintiff in an administrative case may claim compensation for damage caused by an administrative decision.

Suspension of execution of administrative decisions.

Unlawful administrative decisions.

Administrative act [Noun] means an action taken by a state administrative agency or a competent person assigned to perform or not to perform its/his/her tasks or official duties in accordance with law.

Suspension of the performance of administrative acts.

The termination of the administrative act.

The statute of limitations and time limit for issuance of the administrative decision or performance of the administrative act;

Terminate the unlawful administrative act;

Disciplinary [Adjective]: relating to or enforcing discipline.

Dismissal [Noun]: the act of ordering someone to leave.

A disciplinary decision on dismissal.

Lawsuits over disciplinary decisions on dismissal of civil servants.

Internal [Adjective]: existing or occurring inside an organization.

Internal administrative decisions and acts of an agency or organization.

Internal rules of court hearings.

Involved parties [Noun] include the plaintiff, defendant, and persons with related interests and obligations.

Involved parties and defense counsels of their lawful rights and interests shall question witnesses after obtaining the consent of the presiding judge.

Within 3 working days after the conclusion of a court hearing, involved parties shall be provided with judgment extracts by the court.

After issuing a decision to bring the case to trial, the court shall immediately send this decision to involved parties and the same-level procuracy.

Involved parties and the procurator of the same-level procuracy shall be present at the court hearing.

Plaintiff [Noun]: someone or organization that institutes an administrative lawsuit over an administrative decision or act.

The plaintiff and person with related interests and obligations who have independent claims in an administrative case shall pay first-instance legal cost advance.

The plaintiff in an administrative case may claim compensation for damage caused by an administrative decision or act.

The plaintiff that claim compensation for damage shall provide documents and evidences.

Lawful representatives of agencies or organizations that are plaintiffs may make lawsuit petitions by themselves or ask others to do so.

Defendant [Noun] means someone or organization that has made an administrative decision or act.

Defendants have the right to be informed by the court of lawsuits against them;

Person with related interests and obligations means someone or organization that has his/its interests and obligations related to the settlement of an administrative case.

Person with related interests and obligations who have independent claims in an administrative case shall pay first-instance legal cost advance.

Complicated case [Noun] means a case relating to rights and interests of many persons; having contradictory documents and evidences which need examination, verification, assessment or expert opinions; or involving parties who are foreigners.

For a complicated case requiring a prolonged duration of settlement, the chief justice shall assign an alternative judge to ensure the trial is conducted within the time limit prescribed in this Law.

Objective obstacles [Noun] means obstacles caused by objective circumstances rendering persons with interests and obligations unable to know that their lawful rights and interests are infringed upon or to exercise their rights or perform their obligations.

Force Majeure [Noun]: An event occurs in an objective manner which is unforeseeable, unavoidable and unable to be remedied by all possible necessary and admissible measures being taken.

The case in which the plaintiff is absent for force majeure events or objective obstacles.

Legality [Noun]: the state of being legal (something is allowed by the law).

The legality of administrative documents, administrative decisions, administrative acts.

The legality of evidences.

First-instance trial [Noun]: a trial in which legal proceedings are begun or first heard.

The first-instance trial of an administrative case according to summary procedures shall be conducted by a judge.

Appellate court [Noun]: a higher court that is empowered to review decisions of lower courts.

The first-instance and appellate trial regime.

Cassation [Noun]: cancellation; annulment; reversal.

A cassation hearing shall be participated by the same-level procuracy.

Time limit for opening a cassation hearing.

Preparations for a cassation hearing.

Reopening [Noun]: the act of opening again a trial that was closed.

Cassation or reopening procedures.

Persons competent to protest according to reopening procedures:

a) The Chief Justice of the Supreme People's Court;

b) The Procurator General of the Supreme People's Procuracy;

c) Chief justices of superior people's courts;

d) Chief procurators of superior people's procuracies.

People's assessors [Noun]: an adviser or assistant to a judge, especially one serving as a specialist in some field.

Participation of people's assessors in the trial of administrative cases.

When voting on case settlement rulings, people's assessors are equal in power to judges.

Equality [Noun]: the state of being equal, especially in opportunities, status, and rights.

Equality in rights and obligations in administrative procedures

In administrative procedures, everyone is equal before law, regardless of his/her nationality, gender, belief, religion, social stratum, educational level, occupation and social position.

Defense counsel [Noun]: the trial lawyer who is the defendant's representative.

Defense counsels of lawful rights and interests of involved parties.

Involved parties and defense counsels of their lawful rights and interests shall question witnesses after obtaining the consent of the presiding judge.

State secrets [Noun]: issues or information that are kept secret by the government.

State secrets and work secrets.

Procedure-conducting agencies and persons shall keep state secrets and work secrets in accordance with law;

Superior people's courts = high people's court.

Superior people's courts shall supervise trials conducted by lower courts.

Procuracy [Noun]: the office of a procurator.

The procuracy shall consider and handle the case in accordance with the Criminal Procedure Code.

The procuracy may request the court to verify and collect documents and evidences in the course of settlement of a case.

After issuing a decision to bring the case to trial, the court shall immediately send this decision to involved parties and the same-level procuracy.

Procurator [Noun]: one who represents others in a court of law.

Involved parties and the procurator of the same-level procuracy shall be present at the court hearing.

Procurator may produce additional evidences and documents at the appellate court hearing.

Right after the end of the court hearing, the procurator shall send his/her written presentations to the court for the latter to include them in the case file.

A lawsuit [Noun]: This is a claim or complaint against a person or an organization that is made in a court of law by a private person or company.

Order and procedures for instituting lawsuits.

Individuals that institute lawsuits or claim the protection of lawful rights and interests of others have the right and obligation to collect and provide documents and evidences and prove their claims like involved parties.

Lawsuits under the jurisdiction of courts.

The statute of limitations for lawsuit institution.

Petition [Noun]: a formal written request.

Plaintiffs shall send their lawsuit petitions and enclosed documents and evidences to the court.

In case a plaintiff sends a lawsuit petition online, the date of the lawsuit institution is the date of sending the petition.

Court clerk [Noun]: an officer of the court who has responsibilities to maintain records of a court.

A court hearing may be conducted only when it is attended by all members of the trial panel and the court clerk.

The change of a judge, or court clerk will be decided by the chief justice of the court before the opening of a court hearing.

At-law representative = Legal representative [Noun]: a person who represents the legal affairs of another.

Representatives in administrative procedures include at-law representatives and authorized representatives.

The court shall appoint a legal representative of the person with limited legal capacity.

Internal rules of court hearings: a set of rules that govern the internal workings of court hearings.

When participating in procedures, involved parties have obligations to respect the court and strictly observe internal rules of court hearings;

Legal cost = legal expenses [Noun]

To pay legal cost advances, legal cost, fees and other procedural expenses prescribed by law;

Legal cost, fees, and procedural expenses must comply with this Law and the law on legal cost and court fee.

Claim [Noun]: a legal demand; a written request for something.

To maintain, change, add or withdraw their claims;

To change contents of their lawsuit claims within the statute of limitations for lawsuit institution; to withdraw part or the whole of their lawsuit claims.

Authorized representative [Noun]: an individual who represents someone's interests in all aspects of the hearing process.

Representatives in administrative procedures include at-law representatives and authorized representatives.

Authorized representatives in administrative procedures must have the full civil act capacity and be authorized in writing by involved parties or their at-law representatives.

Testimony [Noun]: a formal written or spoken statement that something is true, especially one given in a court of law.

Witnesses have the obligations to:

a) Refuse to make testimonies if their testimonies are related to state secrets, professional secrets, business secrets or privacy secrets or badly or adversely affect involved parties who are their relatives;

b) Pay compensations for damage caused by their untruthful testimonies to involved parties or other persons;

Expert witnesses [Noun]: an individual who is allowed to testify at a trial because of his special knowledge in a particular subject that is relevant to the case.

Expert witnesses are obliged to participate in court hearings when summoned by the court to clarify matters related to the expert examination and expert examination conclusions.

Expert witnesses have the following rights and obligations to be present in response to court summonses and answer questions related to the expert examination;

Urgent measure = immediate measure [Noun]

Application of provisional urgent measures.

When the case has been settled with a legally effective judgment, urgent measures shall be canceled.

Enforcement [Noun]: the act of making people obey a law or rule.

Enforcement of legally effective judgments or rulings.

Evidences = proofs [Noun]

Persons with related interests and obligations are obliged to provide evidences to defend their lawful rights and interests.

Exhibits regarded as evidences must be the original and related to cases or matters being settled.

Evidences are collected from the following sources:

1. Readable, audible or visible materials, or electronic data;

2. Exhibits;

3. Testimonies of involved parties;

4. Testimonies of witnesses;

5. Expert examination conclusions;

6. Written records of on-site appraisal results;

Asset valuation [Noun]: the process of determining the present value of an asset.

Asset valuation and price appraisal results shall be regarded as evidences if the valuation or appraisal is conducted according to procedures prescribed by law.

Involved parties may provide asset prices; or reach agreement on asset valuation and provision of asset prices to the court.

Notarize [Verb]: to have (a document) legalized by a notary.

Notarized or authenticated documents;

Authenticate [Verb]: to prove that (something) is genuine.

Notarized or authenticated documents;

Papers and documents made in a foreign country are notarized or certified in accordance with the law of that country and have been legalized by consular offices;

Evidence forgery [Noun]: the making of a false evidence.

Providers of forged evidences shall compensate for damage in accordance with law if the evidence forgery causes damage to others.

In case the evidence forgery shows signs of a crime, the court shall transfer it to a competent investigative agency for examination.

Preservation [Noun]: the action of preserving something.

Preservation of documents and evidences.

Assessment of evidences [Noun]

The assessment of evidences must be objective, comprehensive, adequate and accurate.

The law on e-transactions.

The provision, delivery or notification of procedural documents through electronic media must comply with the law on e-transactions.

Electronic data messages expressed in the form of exchange of e-data, e-documents, emails, telegrams, facsimiles and other similar forms prescribed by the law on e-transactions.

Trial preparation [Noun]

Time limit for trial preparation.

For complicated cases or due to an objective obstacle, the chief justice of the appellate court may decide to prolong the trial preparation time limit.

Duties and powers of judges in the stage of trial preparation.

Settlement of cases [Noun].

Consequences of the suspension of the settlement of cases.

Termination of the settlement of cases.

Venues of court hearings [Noun].

Court hearings may be held inside or outside courthouses but must ensure the solemnity and decoration of courtrooms.

Direct and oral trial.

The trial shall be conducted orally and proceed in courtrooms.

Postponement [Noun]: the action of postponing something;

Postponement of court hearings.

Suspension [Noun]: the action of suspending someone or something.

Suspension or termination of the settlement of cases at court hearings.

Suspension of the performance of administrative acts.

Suspension of execution of administrative decisions.

Objectivity [Noun]: the state or quality of being objective and fair (based on facts).

Assurance of objectivity of witnesses.

Assurance of impartiality and objectivity in administrative procedures.

Questioning [Noun]: the act of asking someone questions for more information.

Questioning of plaintiffs

Questioning of defendants

Questioning of persons with related interests and obligations

Questioning of witnesses.

Questioning of expert witnesses.

Disclosure [Noun]: the act of revealing secret information.

Disclosure and use of evidences.

Disclosure of documents of cases.

Procedures for disclosure of documents and examination of material exhibits at the hearing.

Examination [Noun]: the act or process of examining something.

Examination of material exhibits.

Examination of evidences.

Appellate trial [Noun]: the retrial of a case by an appellate court.

Guarantee of the first-instance and appellate trial regime.

Notice of payment of legal cost advances for appellate trial.

Acceptance of cases for appellate trial.

Time limit for appellate trial preparation.

Termination of the appellate trial of a case.

Appeal petition [Noun]: a written request to a higher court for a decision of a lower court to be reversed.

An appellant who has the full administrative procedure act capacity may make an appeal petition by himself/herself.

In the bottom of the appeal petition, the appellant shall give his/her signature or fingerprint.

Right after receiving a case file, an appeal petition or a protest decision and enclosed documents and evidences, the appellate court shall record it in the case acceptance book.

Appellant [Noun]: someone who applies a written request to a higher court for a decision of a lower court to be reversed.

When exercising the right to appeal, an appellant shall make an appeal petition.

An appellant who has the full administrative procedure act capacity may make an appeal petition by himself/herself.

Overdue appeals = late appeals [Noun]

A session to examine an overdue appeal shall be attended by the procurator of the same-level procuracy and the person filing the overdue appeal.

The appellate court shall send the decision to the person filing the overdue appeal, same-level procuracy, and first-instance court.

Reopening procedures [Noun]

The time limit for protest according to reopening procedures is one year counting from the date a person competent to protest becomes aware of a ground for protest according to reopening procedures.

Jurisdiction [Noun]: the official power to make or enforce legal decisions and judgments.

Lawsuits under the jurisdiction of courts.

Jurisdiction of the reopening trial panel.

Settlement of disputes over jurisdiction.

Administrative sanction [Noun]: an administrative penalty for disobeying a law or rule.

Administrative sanction without record taking is applicable in cases of warning or fines.

Detoxification [Noun]: medical treatment of a drug addict or alcoholic.

Compulsory detoxification establishments.

Unexpected events [Noun] events that individuals, organizations cannot foresee the consequences of their harmful acts.

Force majeure [Noun]: unforeseeable events that prevent a person from doing something although all necessary measures have been applied.

People without administrative liability capacity are people committing acts of administrative violations while being incapable of cognizing or controlling their acts due to mental disease.

The following case shall not be administratively sanctioned:

The violators do not have administrative liability capacity;

Drug addict [Noun]: a person who uses drugs.

A drug addict who is classified as a dangerous gangster shall be confined to a compulsory educational establishment.

Administrative violation [Noun]: an action that breaks the administrative law.

Principles for handling administrative violations

Intentional administrative violations;

The statute of limitations for handling of administrative violations;

A search of places where material evidences or means of administrative violations are hidden.

Confiscating material evidences and/or means of administrative violations.

Aggravating circumstances [Noun]: circumstances that make an offense more serious/ circumstances that can cause punishment to increase.

The following circumstances are aggravating circumstances:

a) The administrative violations are committed many times or repeated;

b) The administrative violations are committed in an organized manner;

c) Abusing one's positions and powers to commit administrative violations;

Emergency circumstance [Noun]: a situation where there is an immediate threat of death, danger or serious physical harm to a natural person or property.

To combat = to fight [Verb]

Individuals, organizations have responsibilities to combat, prevent and oppose administrative violations.

Forms of administrative sanctions include:

a) Warning;

b) Fines;

c) Confiscating material evidences, means of administrative violation used to commit administrative violations;

e) Expulsion;

Warning shall be applied to people who commit minor administrative violations.

Administrative sanction without record taking is applicable in cases of warning or fines.

If minors are sanctioned with warning, the sanctioning decisions shall be sent to their parents or guardians.

Expulsion means compelling foreigners who have committed acts of administrative violations to leave the territory.

Directors of the Police Departments have rights to decide the expulsion as a sanctioning form.

Forcible [Adjective]: done by force.

Remedial measures include:

a) Forcible restoration of the initial state;

b) Forcible correction of false information or misleading;

Statute of limitations [Noun]: a period of limitation for the bringing of certain kinds of legal action.

Statute of limitations for executing decisions sanctioning administrative violations.

Postponing [Verb]: to put off (something) to a later time;

Postponing execution of decisions on fines.

Time limit postponing the execution of sanctioning decision not exceeding 03 months, as from the day of postponing decision.

Unexpected economic difficulties.

Procedures for paying fines.

Confiscation [Noun]: the action of seizing or taking someone's property.

Confiscation of material evidences or means of administrative violations.

Coercive [Adjective]: using force or threats to persuade people to do something that he is unwilling to do.

Coercive execution of decisions sanctioning administrative violations.

Individuals, organizations receiving the coercive decisions must strictly comply with coercive decisions and be liable to all expenses on the implementation of coercive measures.

The coercive measures include:

The measure of education at communes, wards, district towns

Custody [Noun]: the protective care of something.

Custody of material evidences and/or means of the administrative violations, permits, professional practice certificates according to administrative procedures.

Custody of involved persons according to administrative procedures is just applied in cases need to prevent, stop immediately acts causing a public disturbance, causing injury to other persons.

At the request of the person in custody, the person issuing a decision on custody must notify to his/her family, organization where working or studying thereof.

Remedial [Adjective]: tending to remedy something.

The remedial measure "forcible restoration of the initial state" may apply for minors.

Denunciation [Noun]: an individual notifying a competent organization or individual of a violation committed by any organization or individual which causes or threatens to cause damage to the State interests or legitimate rights and interests of organizations and individuals, including:

a) Denunciation of violations against the law during the performance of duties;

b) Denunciation of violations against the law related to state management of fields;

Denunciations shall be settled in a manner that ensures the safety of the denouncer and protects legitimate rights and interests of the denounced party during the process of settling denunciations.

Denouncer [Noun]: an individual that makes denunciations.

Prohibited acts:

1. Settling denunciations in a negligently and unfair manner.

2. Obstructing and harassing the denouncer.

3. Disclosing the denouncer's name, address, and autograph or other information which may reveal his/her identity.

4. Failing to settle denunciations or deliberately settling denunciations against the law; abusing positions or power to settle denunciations to commit illegal acts or harass denouncing parties and denounced parties.

5. Losing or falsifying case files during the process of settling denunciations.

6. Failure to assume or fully assume the responsibility to protect the denouncer.

7. Threatening, bribing, taking revenge on, victimizing or insulting the denouncer.

8. Illegally interfering with or obstructing denunciation settlement.

9. Protecting the denounced party.

10. Deliberately making untruthful denunciations; forcing, persuading, inciting, counseling and bribing another to make untruthful denunciations; using another person's name to make denunciations.

11. Misusing the denunciation right to oppose or infringe upon the interests of the State; disturbing security and public order; distorting, slandering or harming another person's honor, reputation, and dignity.

12. Bribing, threatening, taking revenge on or insulting denunciation handlers.

13. Providing false information on denunciation and settlement of denunciations.

Rights and obligations of denouncers

1. A denouncer has the rights to:

a) Have his/her name, address, autograph and other personal information kept confidentially;

b) Keep making further denunciation if there are grounds to believe that a competent organization or individual settles the denunciation against the law or a denunciation is yet to be settled within the prescribed limit;

c) Be informed of the acceptance of or failure to accept a denunciation, transfer of his/her denunciation to a competent authority or individual, extension of the time limit for settling the denunciation, termination or suspension of the process of settling the denunciation, continuation in settling the denunciation, and making of conclusions.

d) Withdraw his/her denunciation;

e) Request a competent organization or individual to adopt measures for protecting the denouncer;

f) Be provided with rewards or compensation for any damage he/she incurs as prescribed by law.

A denouncer has the obligations to:

a) Take legal responsibility for the denunciation;

b) Honestly present his/her denunciation; provide his/her information and documents concerning the denunciation.

c) Cooperate with the denunciation handler upon request;

d) Pay compensation for his/her deliberate issuance of untruthful denunciation.

Denounced party [Noun]: an organization or individual whose acts are denounced.

Rights and obligations of the denounced party

A denounced party has the rights to:

a) Be informed of the denunciation, extension of the time limit for settling the denunciation, termination or suspension of the process of settling the denunciation, continuation in settling the denunciation;

b) Have its/his/her legitimate rights and interests protected in case the denunciation handler is yet to give any conclusion about the denunciation.

c) Provide explanation and evidences for untruthful denunciation;

d) Receive denunciation conclusions;

e) Request a competent organization or individual to take actions against any person who deliberately makes an untruthful denunciation or who settles a denunciation against the law;

f) Have its/his/her honor, infringed legitimate rights and interests restored, receive public apologies and corrections and receive compensation for any damage caused by untruthful denunciations or improper settlement of denunciations in accordance with regulations of law.

g) Complain about the settlement decision issued by a competent organization or individual as prescribed by law.

A denounced party has the obligations to:

a) Provide an explanation for the denounced violation; provide relevant information and documents at the request of a competent organization or individual;

b) Be present at the request of the denunciation handler;

c) Strictly comply with the settlement decision according to the conclusion given by the competent organization or individual;

d) Pay compensation for any damages it/he/she inflicts and its/his/her violations against the law.

Denunciation handler [Noun]: an organization or individual that has the power to handle denunciations.

Rights and obligations of denunciation handlers

A denunciation handler has the rights to:

a) Request the denounced party to be present and provide an explanation for the denounced violation; provide information and documents concerning the denunciation;

b) Request the denouncer to be present and provide his/her information and documents concerning the denunciation;

c) Request other organizations and individuals to provide their information and documents concerning the denunciation;

d) Adopt necessary measures to verify and collect information and documents that will be used as the basis for settling denunciations in accordance with regulations of this Law and relevant regulations of law; adopt or request competent organizations and individuals to adopt measures as prescribed by law to prevent or stop the denounced violation;

e) Give a conclusion about the denunciation;

f) Handle the denunciation conclusion within its/his/her power as prescribed by law or request a competent organization or individual to do so.

A denunciation handler has the following obligations:

a) Adopt necessary measures to protect the denouncer within its/his/her power or request a competent authority to do so;

b) Ensure objectiveness, truthfulness, and lawfulness upon denunciation settlement;

c) Do not disclose information about denunciation settlement; protect legitimate rights and interests of the denounced party in case no conclusion is given.

d) Notify the denouncer of the acceptance of or failure to accept the denunciation, transfer of the denunciation to a competent authority or individual, extension of the time limit for settling the denunciation, termination or suspension of the process of settling the denunciation, continuation in settling denunciations, and making of conclusions.

e) Notify the denounced party of the denunciation, extension of the time limit for settling the denunciation, termination or suspension of the process of settling the denunciation, continuation in settling the denunciation; send the denunciation conclusion to the denounce party;

f) Pay compensation for any damages and its/his/her unlawful denunciation settlement.

g) Take legal responsibility for its/his/her denunciation settlement;

Settlement of a denunciation [Noun]: a denunciation handler accepting, verifying, giving and handling conclusions about the denunciation.

During receipt and settlement of a denunciation, if the denounced violation is suspected of a crime, immediately transfer the case file to a competent investigating authority or competent People's Procuracy.

Methods of denunciation:

Denunciation shall be made using a form and directly at a competent authority.

Procedures for settling denunciations

1. Accept a denunciation.

2. Verify the denunciation.

3. Give a conclusion about the denunciation.

4. Handle the denunciation conclusion issued by the denunciation handler.

Accepting denunciations

1. A denunciation handler may issue a denunciation decision if the following conditions are satisfied:

a) The denouncer has the full legal capacity. In the case of limited legal capacity, a representative is required as prescribed by law;

b) The case falls within the recipient's jurisdiction;

c) There are grounds for determining a violator and violation against the law.

2. A decision on denunciation acceptance contains at least:

a) Issuance date of the decision;

b) Grounds for issuing the decision;

c) Accepted denunciation;

d) Time limit for settling the denunciation.

Withdrawal of denunciations

The denouncer may totally or partially withdraw a denunciation before the denunciation handler gives a conclusion on the denunciation. The denunciation shall be withdrawn in writing.

Denunciation resettlement:

A denunciation shall be resettled on one of the following grounds:

a) The result of denunciation verification or conclusion is inaccurate or subjective;

b) Important information, documents and evidences are omitted while verifying or concluding the denunciation;

c) Laws are incorrectly implemented while verifying or concluding the denunciation.

Measures for protecting life, health, property, honor and dignity

1. Take protected persons to a safe place.

2. Provide personnel, vehicles and instruments to directly protect life, health, property, honor and dignity of protected persons in important areas.

3. Adopt necessary measures to prevent and take actions against any infringement upon or threat to life, health, property, honor and dignity of protected persons as prescribed by law.

4. Request persons who infringe upon or threaten life, health, property, honor and dignity of protected persons to stop doing so.

TAX LAW

Personal income tax [Noun]: tax paid on your personal income (the money you earn).

Incomes liable to personal income tax include:

1. Incomes from business activities

2. Incomes from salaries and wages,

3. Incomes from capital investment,

4. Incomes from capital transfer,

5. Incomes from transfer of real estate,

6. Incomes from won prizes,

7. Incomes from copyright.

Taxpayer [Noun]: an individual who has obligation to pay tax.

Personal income taxpayers are people who earn taxable incomes.

A taxable income from inheritance is determined when a taxpayer receives an inherited estate;

A taxable income from gift is determined when a taxpayer is given a gift.

Taxable income [Noun]: the amount of money someone earns used to calculate how much tax he/she has obligation to pay.

Taxable incomes including:

1. Incomes from business activities.

2. Incomes from salaries and wages.

3. Incomes from copyright.

4. Incomes from commercial franchising.

5. Incomes from inheritances that are securities.

6. Incomes from gifts that are securities.

Tax exemption [Noun]: the state of being free from an obligation to pay tax.

Personal income tax exemption or reduction.

Tax reduction [Noun]: the action of allowing someone to pay tax less in amount.

Tax reduction for a taxpayer.

Tax-exempt incomes

Tax-exempt incomes including:

1. Incomes from transfer of residential houses.
2. Incomes from receipt of inheritances or gifts that are real estate.
3. Incomes from scholarships.

Tax declaration [Noun]: a statement made to the tax authorities about the income you have earned during a particular year.

People or organizations that have taxable incomes must have obligations to make tax declaration.

Tax refund [Noun]: the amount of money received back from a tax return.

Individuals are entitled to a tax refund when their taxed incomes do not reach a tax-liable level.

Pre-tax income [Noun]: an income before taxes and deductions.

Pre-tax income from salary, wage or business of a resident taxpayer.

Taxable incomes include:

Income from goods production, business activities and service production.

Income from the right to use assets,

Income from the transfer, or lease of assets,

Income from interests, loans or foreign currency sales.

Tax-exempt incomes.

Taxed income is calculated based on the taxable income minus tax-exempt incomes.

The following goods do not incur export and import duties:

a) Goods in transit;

b) Goods that are humanitarian aid or grant aid;

Free trade zone [Noun]: an area within which goods may be manufactured, handled or transacted without the intervention of the customs authorities.

Goods exported from the domestic market into free trade zones;

Goods imported from free trade zones into the domestic market.

Goods exported from a free trade zone to abroad;

Goods imported from abroad to a free trade zone and used within such free trade zone;

Non-commercial [Adjective]: not intended to make a profit; not having a commercial objective.

Non-commercial goods [Noun]: samples, pictures, videos, models instead of samples; advertisement publications in small quantities.

Non-taxable [Adjective]: incomes or assets on which you do not have to pay tax.

Taxable and non-taxable objects.

Domestically produced goods

The excise taxed price of goods or service is the goods selling price or the service charge, exclusive of excise tax and value-added tax. Specifically:

1. For domestically produced goods, it is the selling price set by the producer;

2. For imported goods eligible for import duty exemption or reduction, it is exclusive of the exempted or reduced import duty amount;

CONCLUSION

Thank you again for downloading this book on *"Administrative and Tax Law in Use: Master 300+ Administrative and Tax Law Terms and Phrases Explained with Examples in 10 Minutes a Day."* and reading all the way to the end. I'm extremely grateful.

If you know of anyone else who may benefit from the essential administrative and tax terms and phrases explained with examples that are revealed in this book, please help me inform them of this book. I would greatly appreciate it.

Finally, if you enjoyed this book and feel that it has added value to your work and study in any way, please take a couple of minutes to share your thoughts and post a REVIEW on Amazon. Your feedback will help me to continue to write other books of law topic that helps you get the best results. Furthermore, if you write a simple REVIEW with positive words for this book on Amazon, you can help hundreds or perhaps thousands of other readers who may want to improve their legal vocabulary so that they could get the greatest achievements in work and study. Like you, they worked hard for every penny they spend on books. With the information and recommendation you provide, they would be more likely to take action right away. We really look forward to reading your review.

Thanks again for your support and good luck!

If you enjoy my book, please write a POSITIVE REVIEW on Amazon.

-- Johnny Chuong --

CHECK OUT OTHER BOOKS

Go here to check out other related books that might interest you:

Legal Vocabulary In Use: Master 600+ Essential Legal Terms And Phrases Explained In 10 Minutes A Day

http://www.amazon.com/dp/B01L0FKXPU

Legal Terminology And Phrases: Essential Legal Terms Explained You Need To Know About Crimes, Penalty And Criminal Procedure

http://www.amazon.com/dp/B01L5EB54Y

Civil Law Vocabulary In Use: Master 350+ Essential Civil Law Terms And Phrases Explained With Examples In 10 Minutes A Day

https://www.amazon.com/dp/B0781TQWGV

Criminal Law Vocabulary In Use: Master 400+ Essential Criminal Law Terms And Phrases Explained With Examples In 10 Minutes A Day https://www.amazon.com/dp/B078KLR51Z

Legal Terminology And Phrases : Master 350+ Essential Business, Enterprise, Commercial and Investment Terms And Phrases Explained With Examples In 10 Minutes A Day.

https://www.amazon.com/dp/B07J3J9Z34

Ielts Academic Vocabulary: Master 3000+ Academic Vocabularies By Topics Explained In 10 Minutes A Day.

https://www.amazon.com/dp/B07F3X3GJ8

IELTS Listening Strategies: The Ultimate Guide with Tips, Tricks and Practice on How to Get a Target Band Score of 8.0+ in 10 Minutes a Day.

https://www.amazon.com/dp/B07845S1MG

IELTS Reading Strategies: The Ultimate Guide with Tips and Tricks on How to Get a Target Band Score of 8.0+ in 10 Minutes a Day.

https://www.amazon.com/dp/B077TWDSJJ

Ielts Writing Task 2 Samples : Over 450 High-Quality Model Essays for Your Reference to Gain a High Band Score 8.0+ In 1 Week (Box set) https://www.amazon.com/dp/B077BYQLPG

Ielts Academic Writing Task 1 Samples: Over 450 High Quality Samples for Your Reference to Gain a High Band Score 8.0+ In 1 Week (Box set) https://www.amazon.com/dp/B077CC5ZG4

Shortcut To English Collocations: Master 2000+ English Collocations In Used Explained Under 20 Minutes A Day (5 books in 1 Box set)

https://www.amazon.com/dp/B06W2P6S22

IELTS Writing Task 1 + 2: The Ultimate Guide with Practice to Get a Target Band Score of 8.0+ In 10 Minutes a Day

https://www.amazon.com/dp/B075DFYPG6

IELTS Speaking Strategies: The Ultimate Guide With Tips, Tricks, And Practice On How To Get A Target Band Score Of 8.0+ In 10 Minutes A Day.

https://www.amazon.com/dp/B075JCW65G

Shortcut To Ielts Writing: The Ultimate Guide To Immediately Increase Your Ielts Writing Scores.

https://www.amazon.com/dp/B01JV7EQGG

Common English Mistakes Explained With Examples: Over 600 Mistakes Almost Students Make and How to Avoid Them in Less Than 5 Minutes A Day

https://www.amazon.com/dp/B072PXVHNZ

Paraphrasing Strategies: 10 Simple Techniques For Effective Paraphrasing In 5 Minutes Or Less

https://www.amazon.com/dp/B071DFG27Q

www.ingramcontent.com/pod-product-compliance
Lightning Source LLC
Chambersburg PA
CBHW030509220526
45464CB00006B/2728